GRAPHING

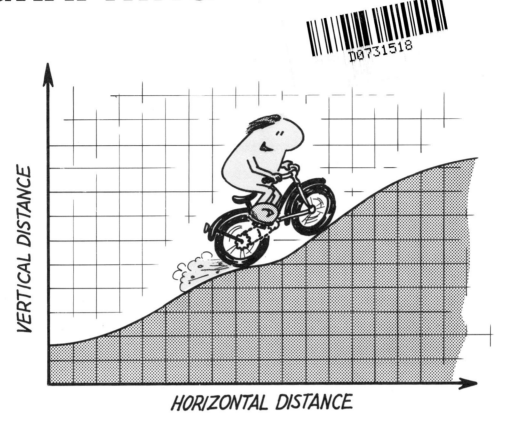

VERTICAL DISTANCE

HORIZONTAL DISTANCE

TASK CARD SERIES

Conceived and
written by
Ron Marson
Illustrated by
Peg Marson

 **TOPS** LEARNING
SYSTEMS

10970 S. Mulino Rd.
Canby OR 97013

ISBN 0-941008-73-8

Printed on Recycled Paper ♻

CONTENTS

PART I — INTRODUCTION

PART II — TEACHING NOTES

PART III — REPRODUCIBLE STUDENT TASK CARDS

A TOPS Model for Effective Science Teaching...

If science were only a set of explanations and a collection of facts, you could teach it with blackboard and chalk. You could assign students to read chapters and answer the questions that followed. Good students would take notes, read the text, turn in assignments, then give you all this information back again on a final exam. Science is traditionally taught in this manner. Everybody learns the same body of information at the same time. Class togetherness is preserved.

But science is more than this.

Science is also process — a dynamic interaction of rational inquiry and creative play. Scientists probe, poke, handle, observe, question, think up theories, test ideas, jump to conclusions, make mistakes, revise, synthesize, communicate, disagree and discover. Students can understand science as process only if they are free to think and act like scientists, in a classroom that recognizes and honors individual differences.

Science is *both* a traditional body of knowledge *and* an individualized process of creative inquiry. Science as process cannot ignore tradition. We stand on the shoulders of those who have gone before. If each generation reinvents the wheel, there is no time to discover the stars. Nor can traditional science continue to evolve and redefine itself without process. Science without this cutting edge of discovery is a static, dead thing.

Here is a teaching model that combines the best of both elements into one integrated whole. It is only a model. Like any scientific theory, it must give way over time to new and better ideas. We challenge you to incorporate this TOPS model into your own teaching practice. Change it and make it better so it works for you.

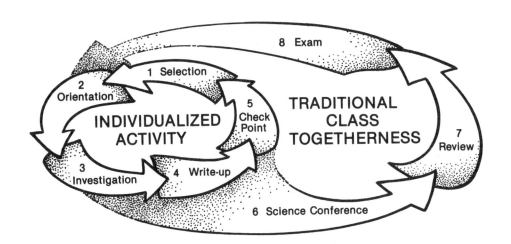

1. SELECTION

Doing TOPS is as easy as selecting the first task card and doing what it says, then the second, then the third, and so on. Working at their own pace, students fall into a natural routine that creates stability and order. They still have questions and problems, to be sure, but students know where they are and where they need to go.

Students generally select task cards in sequence because new concepts build on old ones in a specific order. There are, however, exceptions to this rule: students might *skip* a task that is not challenging; *repeat* a task with doubtful results; *add* a task of their own design to answer original "what would happen if" questions.

2. ORIENTATION

Many students will simply read a task card and immediately understand what to do. Others will require further verbal interpretation. Identify poor readers in your class. When they ask, "What does this mean?" they may be asking in reality, "Will you please read this card aloud?"

With such a diverse range of talent among students, how can you individualize activity and still hope to finish this module as a cohesive group? It's easy. By the time your most advanced students have completed all the task cards, including the enrichment series at the end, your slower students have at least completed the basic core curriculum. This core provides the common background so necessary for meaningful discussion, review and testing on a class basis.

3. INVESTIGATION

Students work through the task cards independently and cooperatively. They follow their own experimental strategies and help each other. You encourage this behavior by helping students only *after* they have tried to help themselves. As a resource person, you work to stay *out* of the center of attention, answering student questions rather than posing teacher questions.

When you need to speak to everyone at once, it is appropriate to interrupt individual task card activity and address the whole class, rather than repeat yourself over and over again. If you plan ahead, you'll find that most interruptions can fit into brief introductory remarks at the beginning of each new period.

4. WRITE-UP

Task cards ask students to explain the "how and why" of things. Write-ups are brief and to the point. Students may accelerate their pace through the task cards by writing these reports out of class.

Students may work alone or in cooperative lab groups. But each one must prepare an original write-up. These must be brought to the teacher for approval as soon as they are completed. Avoid dealing with too many write-ups near the end of the module, by enforcing this simple rule: each write-up must be approved *before* continuing on to the next task card.

5. CHECK POINT

The student and teacher evaluate each write-up together on a pass/no-pass basis. (Thus no time is wasted haggling over grades.) If the student has made reasonable effort consistent with individual ability, the write-up is checked off on a progress chart and included in the student's personal assignment folder or notebook kept on file in class.

Because the student is present when you evaluate, feedback is immediate and effective. A few seconds of this direct student-teacher interaction is surely more effective than 5 minutes worth of margin notes that students may or may not heed. Remember, you don't have to point out every error. Zero in on particulars. If reasonable effort has not been made, direct students to make specific improvements, and see you again for a follow-up check point.

A responsible lab assistant can double the amount of individual attention each student receives. If he or she is mature and respected by your students, have the assistant check the even-numbered write-ups while you check the odd ones. This will balance the work load and insure that all students receive equal treatment.

6. SCIENCE CONFERENCE

After individualized task card activity has ended, this is a time for students to come together, to discuss experimental results, to debate and draw conclusions. Slower students learn about the enrichment activities of faster students. Those who did original investigations, or made unusual discoveries, share this information with their peers, just like scientists at a real conference. This conference is open to films, newspaper articles and community speakers. It is a perfect time to consider the technological and social implications of the topic you are studying.

7. READ AND REVIEW

Does your school have an adopted science textbook? Do parts of your science syllabus still need to be covered? Now is the time to integrate other traditional science resources into your overall program. Your students already share a common background of hands-on lab work. With this shared base of experience, they can now read the text with greater understanding, think and problem-solve more successfully, communicate more effectively.

You might spend just a day on this step or an entire week. Finish with a review of key concepts in preparation for the final exam. Test questions in this module provide an excellent basis for discussion and study.

8. EXAM

Use any combination of the review/test questions, plus questions of your own, to determine how well students have mastered the concepts they've been learning. Those who finish your exam early might begin work on the first activity in the next new TOPS module.

Now that your class has completed a major TOPS learning cycle, it's time to start fresh with a brand new topic. Those who messed up and got behind don't need to stay there. Everyone begins the new topic on an equal footing. This frequent change of pace encourages your students to work hard, to enjoy what they learn, and thereby grow in scientific literacy.

GETTING READY

Here is a checklist of things to think about and preparations to make before your first lesson.

☐ Decide if this TOPS module is the best one to teach next.

TOPS modules are flexible. They can generally be scheduled in any order to meet your own class needs. Some lessons within certain modules, however, do require basic math skills or a knowledge of fundamental laboratory techniques. Review the task cards in this module now if you are not yet familiar with them. Decide whether you should teach any of these other TOPS modules first: *Measuring Length, Graphing, Metric Measure, Weighing* or *Electricity* (before *Magnetism*). It may be that your students already possess these requisite skills or that you can compensate with extra class discussion or special assistance.

☐ Number your task card masters in pencil.

The small number printed in the lower right corner of each task card shows its position within the overall series. If this ordering fits your schedule, copy each number into the blank parentheses directly above it at the top of the card. Be sure to use pencil rather than ink. You may decide to revise, upgrade or rearrange these task cards next time you teach this module. To do this, write your own better ideas on blank 4 x 6 index cards, and renumber them into the task card sequence wherever they fit best. In this manner, your curriculum will adapt and grow as you do.

☐ Copy your task card masters.

You have our permission to reproduce these task cards, for as long as you teach, with only 1 restriction: please limit the distribution of copies you make to the students you personally teach. Encourage other teachers who want to use this module to purchase their *own* copy. This supports TOPS financially, enabling us to continue publishing new TOPS modules for you. For a full list of task card options, please turn to the first task card masters numbered "cards 1-2."

☐ Collect needed materials.

Please see the opposite page.

☐ Organize a way to track completed assignment.

Keep write-ups on file in class. If you lack a vertical file, a box with a brick will serve. File folders or notebooks both make suitable assignment organizers. Students will feel a sense of accomplishment as they see their file folders grow heavy, or their notebooks fill up, with completed assignments. Easy reference and convenient review are assured, since all papers remain in one place.

Ask students to staple a sheet of numbered graph paper to the inside front cover of their file folder or notebook. Use this paper to track each student's progress through the module. Simply initial the corresponding task card number as students turn in each assignment.

☐ Review safety procedures.

Most TOPS experiments are safe even for small children. Certain lessons, however, require heat from a candle flame or Bunsen burner. Others require students to handle sharp objects like scissors, straight pins and razor blades. These task cards should not be attempted by immature students unless they are closely supervised. You might choose instead to turn these experiments into teacher demonstrations.

Unusual hazards are noted in the teaching notes and task cards where appropriate. But the curriculum cannot anticipate irresponsible behavior or negligence. It is ultimately the teacher's responsibility to see that common sense safety rules are followed at all times. Begin with these basic safety rules:

1. Eye Protection: Wear safety goggles when heating liquids or solids to high temperatures.
2. Poisons: Never taste anything unless told to do so.
3. Fire: Keep loose hair or clothing away from flames. Point test tubes which are heating away from your face and your neighbor's.
4. Glass Tubing: Don't force through stoppers. (The teacher should fit glass tubes to stoppers in advance, using a lubricant.)
5. Gas: Light the match first, before turning on the gas.

☐ Communicate your grading expectations.

Whatever your philosophy of grading, your students need to understand the standards you expect and how they will be assessed. Here is a grading scheme that counts individual effort, attitude and overall achievement. We think these 3 components deserve equal weight:

1. Pace (effort): Tally the number of check points you have initialed on the graph paper attached to each student's file folder or science notebook. Low ability students should be able to keep pace with gifted students, since write-ups are evaluated relative to individual performance standards. Students with absences or those who tend to work at a slow pace may (or may not) choose to overcome this disadvantage by assigning themselves more homework out of class.

2. Participation (attitude): This is a subjective grade assigned to reflect each student's attitude and class behavior. Active participators who work to capacity receive high marks. Inactive onlookers, who waste time in class and copy the results of others, receive low marks.

3. Exam (achievement): Task cards point toward generalizations that provide a base for hypothesizing and predicting. A final test over the entire module determines whether students understand relevant theory and can apply it in a predictive way.

Gathering Materials

Listed below is everything you'll need to teach this module. You already have many of these items. The rest are available from your supermarket, drugstore and hardware store. Laboratory supplies may be ordered through a science supply catalog. Hobby stores also carry basic science equipment.

Keep this classification key in mind as you review what's needed:

special in-a-box materials:	general on-the-shelf materials:
Italic type suggests that these materials are unusual. Keep these specialty items in a separate box. After you finish teaching this module, label the box for storage and put it away, ready to use again the next time you teach this module.	Normal type suggests that these materials are common. Keep these basics on shelves or in drawers that are readily accessible to your students. The next TOPS module you teach will likely utilize many of these same materials.
(substituted materials):	*optional materials:
A parentheses following any item suggests a ready substitute. These alternatives may work just as well as the original, perhaps better. Don't be afraid to improvise, to make do with what you have.	An asterisk sets these items apart. They are nice to have, but you can easily live without them. They are probably not worth an extra trip, unless you are gathering other materials as well.

Everything is listed in order of first use. Start gathering at the top of this list and work down. Ask students to bring recycled items from home. The teaching notes may occasionally suggest additional student activity under the heading "Extensions." Materials for these optional experiments are listed neither here nor in the teaching notes. Read the extension itself to find out what new materials, if any, are required.

Needed quantities depend on how many students you have, how you organize them into activity groups, and how you teach. Decide which of these 3 estimates best applies to you, then adjust quantities up or down as necessary:

$Q_1 / Q_2 / Q_3$

Single Student: Enough for 1 student to do all the experiments.
Individualized Approach: Enough for 30 students informally working in 10 lab groups, all self-paced.
Traditional Approach: Enough for 30 students, organized into 10 lab groups, all doing the same lesson.

KEY:	*special in-a-box materials*	general on-the-shelf materials
	(substituted materials)	*optional materials

$Q_1 / Q_2 / Q_3$

1 / 10 / 10	textbooks with a least 400 pages
2 / 20 / 20	index cards — 4x6 or larger
1 / 10 / 10	pairs of scissors
1 / 1 / 1	spools of thread
1 / 1 / 1	roll masking tape
1 / 5 / 10	100 ml graduated cylinders
1 / 20 / 30	100 ml beakers
1 / 10 / 10	large test tubes with 20-30 ml capacities
1 / 5 / 10	*drinking glasses that taper outward — clear plastic disposable beverage cups often have this shape; choose the most exaggerated style*
1 / 5 / 10	Erlenmeyer flasks, 100 ml or larger
.3 / 1 / 3	cups oil-based clay
1 / 5 / 10	small test tubes with 5-10 ml capacities
4 / 20 / 40	*cylinders of various sizes and kinds, including cans bottles and lids*
1 / 1 / 1	roll string
1 / 5 / 10	*hand calculators
1 / 5 / 10	soup cans or equivalent size
1 / 10 / 10	thin rubber bands of uniform thickness, about 6 cm long
2 / 20 / 20	paper clips
1 / 10 / 10	pieces lined notebook paper
1 / 20 / 30	metric rulers
1 / 4 / 10	*chrome-plated tubing at least one inch in diameter or larger*

Sequencing Task Cards

This logic tree shows how all the task cards in this module tie together. In general, students begin at the trunk of the tree and work up through the related branches. As the diagram suggests, the way to upper level activities leads up from lower level activities.

At the teacher's discretion, certain activities can be omitted or sequences changed to meet specific class needs. The only activities that must be completed in sequence are indicated by leaves that open *vertically* into the ones above them. In these cases the lower activity is a prerequisite to the upper.

When possible, students should complete the task cards in the same sequence as numbered. If time is short, however, or certain students need to catch up, you can use the logic tree to identify concept-related *horizontal* activities. Some of these might be omitted since they serve only to reinforce learned concepts rather than introduce new ones.

On the other hand, if students complete all the activities at a certain horizontal concept level, then experience difficulty at the next higher level, you might go back down the logic tree to have students repeat specific key activities for greater reinforcement.

For whatever reason, when you wish to make sequence changes, you'll find this logic tree a valuable reference. Parentheses in the upper right corner of each task card allow you total flexibility. They are left blank so you can pencil in sequence numbers of your own choosing.

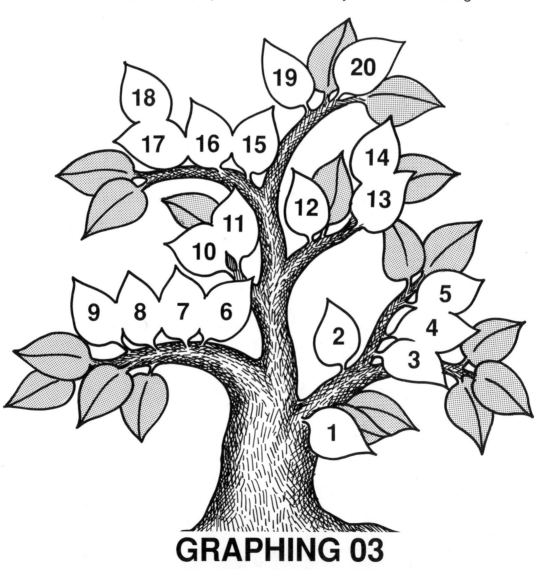

GRAPHING 03

E

LONG-RANGE
OBJECTIVES

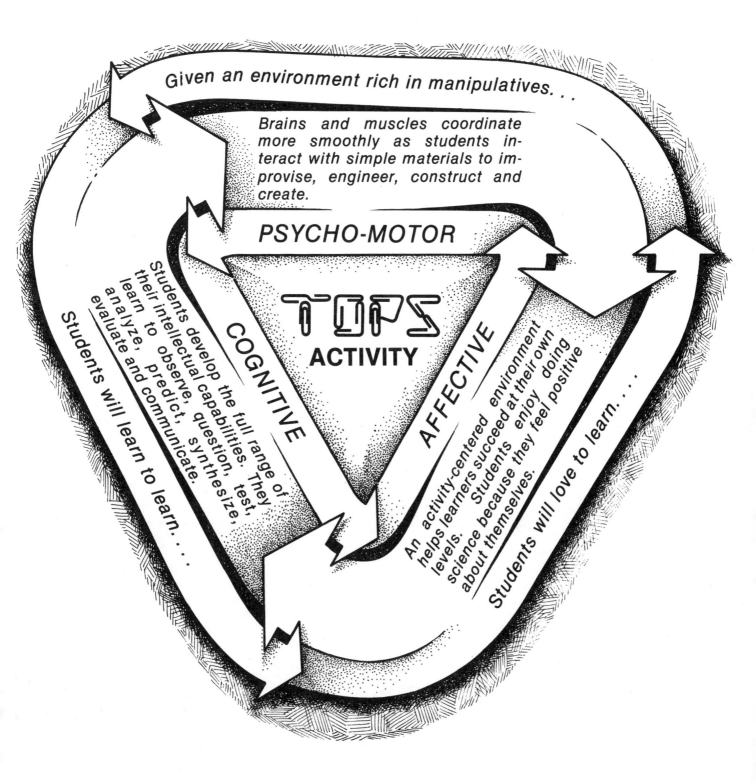

Given an environment rich in manipulatives. . .

Brains and muscles coordinate more smoothly as students interact with simple materials to improvise, engineer, construct and create.

PSYCHO-MOTOR

TOPS ACTIVITY

Students develop the full range of their intellectual capabilities. They learn to observe, question, test, analyze, predict, synthesize, evaluate and communicate.

COGNITIVE

AFFECTIVE

An activity-centered environment helps learners succeed at their own levels. Students enjoy doing science because they feel positive about themselves.

Students will learn to learn. . . .

Students will love to learn. . . .

Review / Test Questions

Photocopy the questions below. On a separate sheet of blank paper, cut and paste those boxes you want to use as test questions. Include questions of your own design, as well. Crowd all these questions onto a single page for students to answer on separate pieces of graph paper. Duplicate a class set and your custom-made test is ready to use. Use leftover questions as a review in preparation for the final exam.

task 1
Draw a pair of coordinates on graph paper. Then draw a straight line from (2,1) to (5,8) to (8,1) to (1,5) to (9,5) to (2,1). What have you drawn?

task 2
Draw these coordinates as scaled. Plot the points in this data table and draw a suitable graph line.

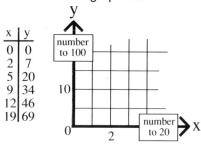

x	y
0	0
2	7
5	20
9	34
12	46
19	69

task 3-5
A stack of 6 quarters measures 1 cm high.
a. Fill in this table and graph your results.

number of quarters	height (cm)
0	0
6	
12	
18	

b. Banks sell quarters in 10 dollar rolls. Use your graph to predict the length of each roll.

task 4
a. Extrapolate the graph (directly above) to find how many quarters form a stack 35 cm high.
b. Prove your extrapolation is correct by solving this proportion:

$$\frac{1 \text{ cm}}{6 \text{ quarters}} = \frac{35 \text{ cm}}{?}$$

task 6-9
This graph shows how the height of water in 4 bottles varies with the volume of water added. Draw each bottle, giving reasons for the shapes you choose.

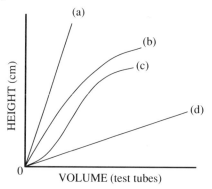

task 10-11
For each table, decide by graphing if **x** is directly proportional to **y**. Use math to show you are correct.

(a)
x	y
0	0
5	2.5
12	6
13	6.5
18	9

(b)
x	y
0	0
5	1
9	2
12	5
14	9

task 12
a. Circle A has a circumference of 19 cm. Use the pi graph to find its diameter.
b. Circle B has a diameter of 3 cm. Use the pi graph to find its circumference.

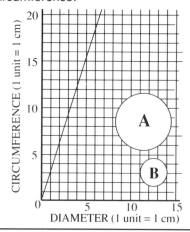

task 13-14
The graph shows how 2 pairs of rubber bands stretch as weight is added.

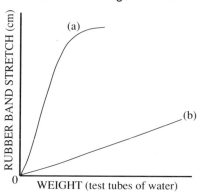

a. Which graph line represents 2 rubber bands connected in parallel (side by side)? Explain.
b. Which graph line represents 2 rubber bands connected in series (end to end)? Explain.
c. Which graph line indicates that the rubber bands may soon break? Explain.

task 15-18
Change the scale on either the x-axis or the y-axis to transform this rectangle into a square.

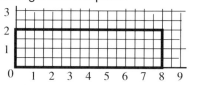

task 19-20
A certain one-celled organism divides every hour. Starting with just 1 organism at time zero, graph the total population of cells over a 12 hour period.

Answers

task 1
The points connect to form a star.

task 2

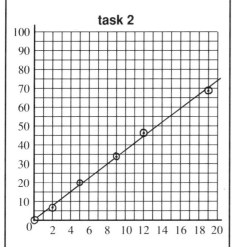

task 3-5

a.

quarters	ht (cm)
0	0
6	1
12	2
18	3
24	4
30	5

b. 40 quarters make $10. The graph line crosses the 40 quarter mark at about 6.7 cm.

task 4

a.

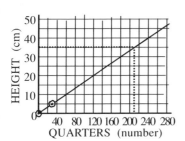

At 35 cm of quarters, the graph line extends to about 208 quarters.

b. 1 cm x ? = 35 cm x 6 quarters
        ? = 210 quarters
This is in close agreement with the extrapolation in part (a).

task 6-9

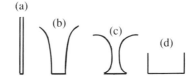

a. A straight graph line indicates a bottle with uniform diameter. It extends highest up the vertical axis, so it must be the tallest.

b. The graph line curves down into an ever more gentle slope, indicating a diameter that widens from the base.

c. The graph line first curves up, suggesting a narrowing diameter. Then it straightens and curves down, implying an elongated hour-glass shape.

d. A straight line suggests a bottle with uniform diameter. The shallow slope extends far out the horizontal axis, implying the bottle has a large volume capacity, but remains short.

task 10-11

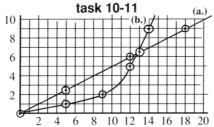

Only in table (a) is **x** proportional to **y**. Its points graph into a straight line, and the ratio of its coordinates (y/x) is a constant 1/2:

5/2.5 = 6/12 = 13/6.5 = 9/18.

The ratio of ordered pairs in (b), by contrast, is not constant:

1/5 ≠ 2/9 ≠ 5/12 ≠ 9/14.

task 12

a. Diameter of A = 6.1 cm. (19 cm on the y axis meets the pi graph at just over 6 cm on the x axis.)

b. Circumference of B = 9.4 cm (3 cm on the x axis meets the pi graph between 9 and 10 cm on the y axis.)

task 13-14

a. Shallow graph line (b) represents rubber bands that are connected in parallel. Each band supports only half the load. Together they stretch half as far as they would if acting alone.

b. Steep graph line (a) represents rubber bands that are connected in series. Each rubber band stretches farther because it supports the full load. And because these increases add together, there is a 4-fold increase over (b).

c. Graph line (a) seems most likely to break. The flattening at the top of its curve indicates that it has little capacity to stretch further.

task 15-18
(Here the y axis is expanded four times.)

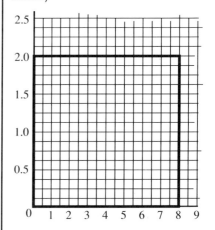

task 19-20

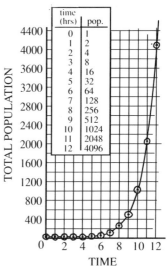

time (hrs)	pop.
0	1
1	2
2	4
3	8
4	16
5	32
6	64
7	128
8	256
9	512
10	1024
11	2048
12	4096

TEACHING NOTES
For Activities 1-20

Task Objective (TO) practice plotting ordered pairs of whole numbers on a coordinate system.

ORDERED PAIRS (1)   O   Graphing (   )

1. Draw X and Y coordinates on graph paper. Number alternate lines out to 10 as shown.

2. Plot the ordered pairs listed in each table. Connect points, working down from the top of each table.

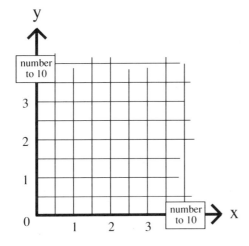

(a)		(b)	
x	y	x	y
5	5	5	9
5	0	4	8
4	2	3	8
3	3	4	7
3	2	3	6
5	0	4	6
6	3	5	5
7	4	6	6
7	3	7	6
5	0	6	7
		7	8
		6	8
		5	9

(c)
Make a circle with the center at (5,7) and a radius of 1.

3. What have you drawn?

1

Answers / Notes

1-3. *The points connect to form a flower.*

Students should save their graph for later reference. In task cards 15-17 they will transform the shape of their flower by mapping its ordered pairs onto other coordinate systems.

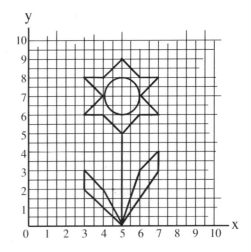

Materials

☐ Graph paper for students to cut apart as needed. Use your own, or photocopy the grid at the back of this book. (Your class will require 10-15 sheets per student, depending on how well they conserve paper and how large they scale their graphs. Run off 10 sheets to start. Photocopy the balance when more exact needs become apparent.)

(TO) plot ordered pairs on coordinate systems with different scales. To practice estimating between graph lines when placing points.

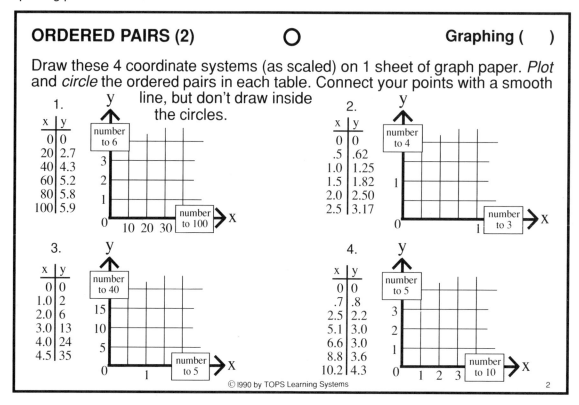

ORDERED PAIRS (2) ○ **Graphing ( )**

Draw these 4 coordinate systems (as scaled) on 1 sheet of graph paper. *Plot* and *circle* the ordered pairs in each table. Connect your points with a smooth line, but don't draw inside the circles.

1.

x	y
0	0
20	2.7
40	4.3
60	5.2
80	5.8
100	5.9

number to 6
number to 100

2.

x	y
0	0
.5	.62
1.0	1.25
1.5	1.82
2.0	2.50
2.5	3.17

number to 4
number to 3

3.

x	y
0	0
1.0	2
2.0	6
3.0	13
4.0	24
4.5	35

number to 40
number to 5

4.

x	y
0	0
.7	.8
2.5	2.2
5.1	3.0
6.6	3.0
8.8	3.6
10.2	4.3

number to 5
number to 10

© 1990 by TOPS Learning Systems

2

Introduction

Draw figures like these on your blackboard. Discuss where the question mark falls.

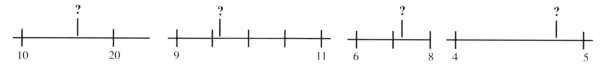

Answers / Notes

Graphs with these scales are typical of many that students will encounter throughout this module. Extra practice now in accurately plotting points will insure better results later.

1.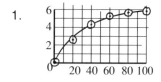

2.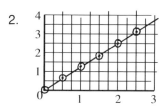

3.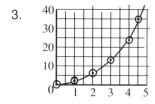

4.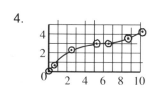

Materials

☐ Graph paper.

(TO) graph how the thickness of a book increases with its number of leaves.

BOOK LEAVES (1)   ◯   Graphing (   )

1. Select a book with at least 200 leaves (400 pages). Complete the data table by counting leaves and measuring their thickness in millimeters. Estimate between the lines to the nearest 0.1 mm.

2. Plot and circle each ordered pair. Connect your points with a straight line, but don't draw inside the circles.

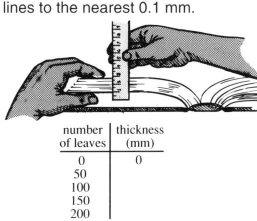

number of leaves	thickness (mm)
0	0
50	
100	
150	
200	

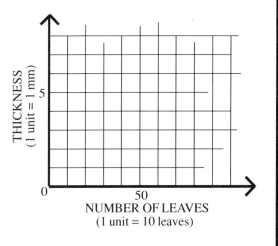

3

Introduction

(a) Illustrate how to measure paper thickness in a book so that each leaf is stacked vertically over the page beneath without fanning out.

(b) Ask students to measure the thickness of 75 leaves (150 pages) in one of their text books, a math book perhaps. (Check in advance to make sure this many pages falls *between* the mm divisions on your ruler. If the measurement falls *on* a mm division, assign a different number of pages to measure.) Ask each student to write the result on a slip of paper and turn it in. Write each measurement on your blackboard and analyze the results: Cross out answers that are just plain wrong. Notice how those that are left all agree in the units place, because this figure is certain. Answers disagree in the tenths place because the figure is estimated, and therefore uncertain.

Answers / Notes

1-2. *The slope, a function of paper thickness, may differ from this example.*

number of leaves	0	50	100	150	200
thickness (mm)	0	3.8	7.2	10.6	14.1

Materials

☐ A book with at least 200 leaves (400 pages). If you assign students to use a specific textbook, all graphs will be uniform.

☐ A centimeter ruler that has mm subdivisions. Use metric lab rulers. Or supply photocopies of the line master from the back of this book, and scissors to cut out just one of the ruler images. Direct students to save the other rulers on this page to use in later experiments.

☐ Graph paper.

☐ A straight edge.

(TO) compare data that is read from a graph with actual measurements. To interpret the physical significance of the slope.

BOOK LEAVES (2) ◯ Graphing ( )

1. Read from your graph the number of leaves in 10.0 mm. Check your answer by counting book leaves. How do your answers compare?

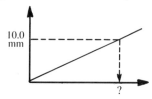

2. Read from your graph the thickness of 25 leaves. Check your answer by actual measurement. How do your answers compare?

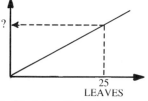

3. Divide 2 index cards into 25 rectangles each. Stack them to form a flat, even edge, then rubber-band them together.

50 LAYERS

4. Plot and label a graph line for index cards on your book-leaves graph. Extrapolate (extend) the line past 50 leaves.

5. How is the slope (steepness) of the graph line related to paper thickness?

4

Answers / Notes

1. *Agreement that is too good to be true probably is. Commend students for reporting what they actually measured, not what they wished they had measured. An uncertainty of 10 book leaves is not unreasonable when measuring relatively thin paper. Here is one result:*

    graph prediction = 140 book leaves
    measuring 10.0 mm of leaves and counting = 144

2. *Agreement should be within .1 or .2 mm. Here is one result:*

    graph prediction = 1.8 mm
    counting 25 leaves and measuring = 2.0

4. *No leaves have no thickness. This zero graph point, plus a second graph point determined by the thickness of 50 index cards (9.9 mm in our particular case), define the straight line.*

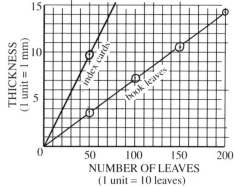

5. The thicker the paper, the steeper the slope. The index-card graph line rises far more steeply than the textbook paper graph line because the paper is much thicker.

Materials

☐ The same book that was measured in the previous activity and its accompanying graph.
☐ Index cards, 4x6 inch or larger.
☐ A pair of scissors.
☐ A straight edge.

(TO) extrapolate straight line graphs. To check the validity of each extension mathematically.

EXTRAPOLATING BOOK LEAVES

○   **Graphing ( )**

1. Draw a new graph with a scale that is 5 times smaller. Plot the same points you measured in activities 3 and 4.

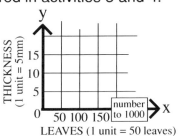

2. Extrapolate your graph lines out to 1000 leaves. Use thread to help you judge the best direction. Label both graph lines.

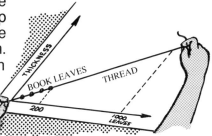

3. Read your graph to find the thickness of 1000 book leaves and 1000 index cards.

4. Check each answer by solving these proportions. Why don't your extrapolations exactly agree with your calculations?

BOOK LEAVES

$$\frac{200 \text{ leaves}}{\text{thickness}} = \frac{1000 \text{ leaves}}{?}$$

└─ *(Use measurement from activity 3.)*

INDEX CARD

$$\frac{50 \text{ leaves}}{\text{thickness}} = \frac{1000 \text{ leaves}}{?}$$

└─ *(Use measurement from activity 4.)*

5

Answers / Notes

3. This extrapolated graph shows that
   1000 book leaves = 72 mm
   1000 index cards = 208 mm

4. Using cross multiplication,
   Book Leaves: 200 leaves x ? = 1000 leaves x 14.1 mm
                    ? = 14.1 mm x 1000/200 = 70.5 mm
   Index Cards: 50 leaves x ? = 1000 leaves x 9.9 mm
                    ? = 9.9 mm x 1000/50 = 198.0 mm

Agreement is reasonably close, but not exact. A small misalignment of an extrapolated line will significantly multiply error as it is extended.

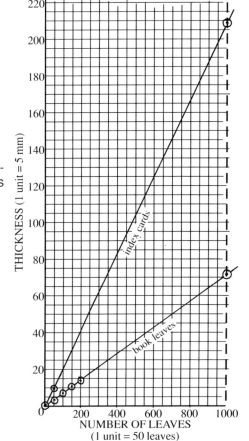

Materials

☐ Graph paper.
☐ Thread.
☐ A straight edge.
☐ Data from activities 3 and 4.

(TO) graph how the height of water in uniform cylinders changes with increasing volume.

CONTAINER CURVES (1)   ○   Graphing (   )

1. Cut out 2 metric rulers. Fix 1 each to a 100 ml graduate and a 100 ml beaker resting on a flat surface.

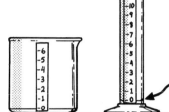

a. Trim excess ruler off the top …

b. Fix the back of the ruler to the glass with masking tape rolled sticky side out …

c. Add just enough water to form a water line., Fix "0" on the ruler over this line.

2. Pour large test tubes full of water into each container. Record the height of the water level after each addition in a data table.

3. Plot your data for both containers onto the same graph. Label each graph line.

4. Why is the slope of one graph line steeper than the other?

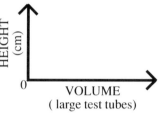

HEIGHT (cm)

0   VOLUME
(large test tubes)

6

Introduction

If your students are unpracticed at reading accurate water levels, show by diagram how water curves against glass to form a meniscus. Demonstrate how to align the bottom of this curve to the ruler, always viewing the meniscus at eye level to avoid parallax. With care, the ruler can be read to the nearest .01 cm, although there is considerable uncertainty in the hundredths place.

Answers / Notes

2-3.

VOLUME (in large test tubes)	HEIGHT (cm) beaker	cylinder
0	0	0
1	1.65	5.30
2	3.30	10.75
3	5.05	16.25

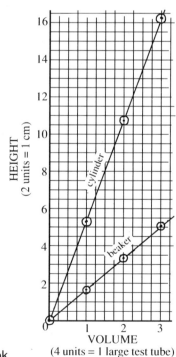

HEIGHT (2 units = 1 cm)

cylinder

beaker

VOLUME
(4 units = 1 large test tube)

4. The graph line for the graduated cylinder is steeper than the graph line for the beaker because it has a smaller diameter. Test tubes of water fill the narrower cylinder much faster than the broader beaker.

Materials

☐ Paper rulers photocopied from the line master at the back of this book.

☐ Scissors and masking tape.

☐ A 100 ml graduated cylinder and a 100 ml beaker.

☐ A large test tube, or equivalent, to measure out water in 20 to 30 ml increments. Our particular test tube was 15 cm long and held 29 ml of water. Limit all "large" test tubes in your class to just one particular size.

☐ If water sources are not well distributed around your room, supply buckets.

☐ Graph paper and a straight edge.

(TO) graph how the height of water in non-uniform cylinders changes with increasing volume.

CONTAINER CURVES (2)   Graphing (   )

1. Collect containers shaped like those below.

2. Tape rulers to the sides of each one as before. Record how the water level rises in each container as you add test tubes of water. Graph your results.

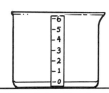
Straight Beaker

Tapered Glass

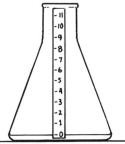
Erlenmeyer Flask

3. Explain how the graph line of each container is determined by its three-dimensional shape.

7

Answers / Notes

1-2.

VOLUME (in large test tubes)	DISTANCE UP CONTAINER (cm)		
	straight beaker	tapered glass	Erlenmeyer flask
0	0	0	0
1	1.65	1.18	1.05
2	3.30	2.11	2.28
3	5.05	3.00	3.62
4		3.73	5.25
5		4.41	10.55
6		5.10	
7		5.61	
8		6.20	

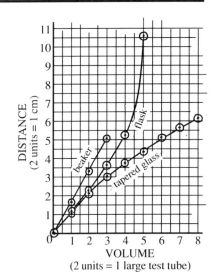

3. STRAIGHT BEAKER: Because this container has the shape of a uniform cylinder, each test tube of water will raise the water level by a constant amount, forming a uniform straight line.

TAPERED GLASS: Because this container tapers outward, its capacity to hold water steadily increases as the water level rises. Thus each test tube of water raises the water level by a decreasing amount, causing the graph line to curve down.

ERLENMEYER FLASK: Because this container tapers inward, its capacity to hold water steadily decreases as the water level rises. Thus each test tube of water raises the water level by an increasing amount, causing the graph line to curve up. Near the top of the bottle, it straightens into a narrow uniform cylinder.

Materials

☐ A beaker. Use the same 100 ml beaker as before.
☐ A glass that tapers outward. Containers of this shape are often sold as clear plastic disposable beverage cups in grocery stores.
☐ An Erlenmeyer flask, 100 ml or larger. We used a 125 ml flask.

☐ Paper rulers, scissors and masking tape.
☐ A large test tube or equivalent to measure out water. Use the same capacity as before.
☐ Graph paper and a straight edge.

(TO) graph how the height of water in non-empty containers changes with increasing volume.

CONTAINER CURVES (3)　　　　O　　　　Graphing (　)

1. Set up 100 ml beakers like these. Make the ball out of clay. Roll it to fit inside the beaker with about 1/2 cm to spare.

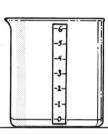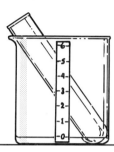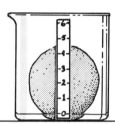

No Object　　　　Large Test Tube　　　　Clay Ball

2. What shape do you think the graph lines will take as you fill these containers? Draw your best guess *before* you experiment.

3. Now do the experiment. This time add small test tubes of water, in place of large ones. Evaluate your prediction.

　　　　8

Answers / Notes

1. *If glassware is in short supply, use just one beaker for all 3 trials.*
2. *Important elements to consider when predicting the graph line are its basic shape (straight?, upward curve?, downward curve?), and its extension along each axis.*
3. *In this activity, a small test tube is used to measure water instead of a large one. This insures that the beakers will not fill so rapidly that the shape of the clay ball is poorly defined. Neither the ball nor the test tube should touch the side of the beaker that is nearest the ruler, since they distort the water line at their point of contact.*

VOLUME (in small test tubes)	HEIGHT OF BEAKER (cm) with… no object	test tube	clay ball
0	0	0	0
1	0.52	0.52	1.10
2	1.05	1.19	2.73
3	1.60	1.85	3.56
4	2.16	2.52	4.10
5	2.70	3.20	4.68
6	3.22	3.87	5.20
7	3.80	4.50	
8	4.34	5.15	
9	4.92	5.80	
10	5.47		

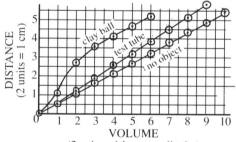

Remind students to evaluate their predictions. Require a more sophisticated analysis than "I was right" or "I was wrong."

Materials

- ☐ Three 100 ml beakers.
- ☐ A large test tube.
- ☐ Oil-based clay.
- ☐ Paper rulers.
- ☐ Scissors.
- ☐ Masking tape.

- ☐ A small test tube, or equivalent, to measure out water in 5 to 10 ml increments. Our particular test tube was 10 cm long and held 9 ml of water. Limit all "small" test tubes in your class to one particular size.
- ☐ Graph paper.
- ☐ A straight edge.

(TO) summarize the physical significance of graph lines as they relate to containers of various sizes and shapes.

SQUARES OF WATER   Graphing (   )

1. Graph each shape on the same grid. (Hint: Think about adding "squares" of water.)

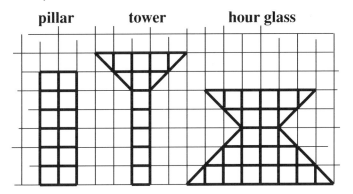

pillar   tower   hour glass

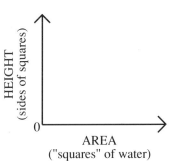

2. Explain how your graph lines indicate…

   a. the tallest shape.   d. a widening shape.
   b. the largest shape.   e. a uniform shape.
   c. a narrowing shape.

9

Answers / Notes

1. *This activity should engage the mind more than the hands.*

pillar			tower			hour glass	
A	h		A	h		A	h
2	1		1	1		7	1
4	2		2	2		12	2
6	3		3	3		15	3
8	4		4	4		18	4
10	5		5	5		23	5
12	6		7	6			
			11	7			

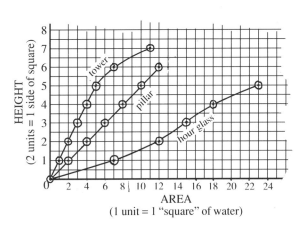

2a. The graph line for the tallest shape (the tower), extends highest up the vertical axis.
2b. The graph line for the largest shape (the hour glass), extends farthest out the horizontal axis.
2c. When a shape narrows (the hour glass), its graph line curves up.
2d. When a shape widens (the tower and the hour glass), its graph line curves down.
2e. If a shape is uniform (the pillar and bottom part of the tower), its graph line is straight.

Materials

☐ Graph paper.
☐ A straight edge.

(TO) discover that the ratio of coordinates (y/x) is constant for points that lie on any common straight line intersecting (0,0).

WHAT'S THE POINT? ◯ Graphing ( )

1a. Divide the y coordinate of each point by it x coordinate (y/x). List your results.

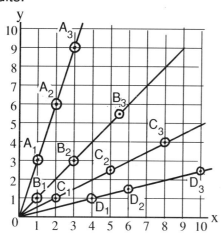

2a. Find the ratio of coordinates (y/x) for each point on these curves. List your results.

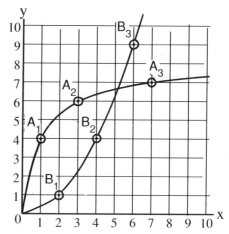

1b. If points lie on the same straight line, what seems true?

2b. What can you conclude?

10

Answers / Notes

1a.
$$A_1 = 3/1 = 3 \qquad B_1 = 1/1 = 1$$
$$A_2 = 6/2 = 3 \qquad B_2 = 3/3 = 1$$
$$A_3 = 9/3 = 3 \qquad B_3 = 5.5/5.5 = 1$$

$$C_1 = 1/2 = .5 \qquad D_1 = 1/4 = .25$$
$$C_2 = 2.5/5 = .5 \qquad D_2 = 1.5/6 = .25$$
$$C_3 = 4/8 = .5 \qquad D_3 = 2.5/10 = .25$$

2a.
$$A_1 = 4/1 = 4 \qquad B_1 = 1/2 = .5$$
$$A_2 = 6/3 = 2 \qquad B_2 = 4/4 = 1$$
$$A_3 = 7/7 = 1 \qquad B_3 = 9/6 = 1.5$$

1b. If points lie on the same straight line that intersects (0,0), the ratio of their coordinates (y/x) seems to be constant.

2b. If points lie on a common curve, the ratio of their coordinates (y/x) will change.

Materials

None.

(TO) decide by graphing if two variables are directly proportional.

DIRECTLY PROPORTIONAL? ○   Graphing (   )

1. Decide by graphing if the side of a square is directly proportional to its...

...area.   ...perimeter.

LENGTH (sides)	AREA (squares)
1	1 □
2	4 ⊞
3	9 ▦
4	16 ▦

LENGTH (sides)	PERIMETER (sides)
1	4 □
2	8 ⊞
3	12 ▦
4	16 ▦

2. What can you conclude?

11

Answers / Notes

1.

LENGTH (sides)	AREA (squares)	PERIMETER (sides)
0	0	0
1	1	4
2	4	8
3	9	12
4	16	16
5	25	20
6	36	24
7	49	28
8	64	32
9	81	36
10	100	40

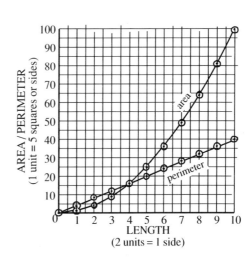

2. AREA: The curved graph line shows that the side of a square is not proportional to its area. The ratios of the coordinates (area/length) at each point on the line vary: $1/1 \neq 4/2 \neq 9/3$, etc.

PERIMETER: The straight graph line shows that the side of a squares is proportional to its perimeter. The ratios of the coordinates (perimeter/length) at each point on the line are constant: $4/1 = 8/2 = 12/3$, etc.

Discussion

How would you use the area graph to find square roots?

Materials

□ Graph paper.
□ A straight edge.

(TO) graph how the diameter of a cylinder is related to its circumference.

PI GRAPH Graphing (   )

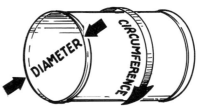

1. Measure the diameter and circumference of 4 different cylinders. Use bottles, cans, lids or other circular objects.

2. Complete this data table. Draw a straight line between your points, using thread to help you determine its best placement.

kind of CYLINDER	DIAMETER (cm)	CIRCUMFERENCE (cm)

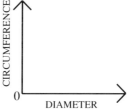

3. What is the ratio of coordinates (C/d) for all points on this line? Explain.

4. These equations are famous in geometry: π = C/d, C = πd, d = C/π. What do they mean?

12

Answers / Notes

1-2. Students must estimate between the lines on both axes to place their graph points. To simplify this task, both the x and y axis are here held to the same scale (1 unit = 1 cm), even though this creates an unusually long graph.

kind of CYLINDER	DIAMETER (cm)	CIRCUMFERENCE (cm)
pill container	2.41	7.9
drinking glass	7.75	24.6
tuna fish can	8.48	27.1
large oatmeal box	13.51	42.9

3. The ratio (3.1) is the same for all points on the graph line. *Students can simplify their arithmetic, therefore, by choosing points that have coordinates with easily divisible denominators: (3.1, 1), (6.3, 2) and (31.4, 10).*

4. The circumference of any circle divided by its diameter always yields the same constant result. The Greeks called it "pi." Given the diameter of a circle, multiply by π to find the circumference; given the circumference, divide by π to find the diameter.

Materials

☐ Cylindrical objects (cans, bottles, lids, pipe, coins, etc,) of 4 different sizes. Include at least 1 small cylinder and 1 large cylinder.
☐ String to measure the circumference of each cylinder. Or students might roll the cylinder one complete revolution (without allowing it to slip), and measure the distance traveled.
☐ A ruler and thread.
☐ Graph paper.

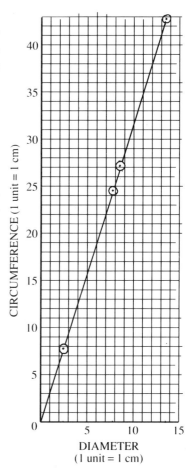

(TO) graph how a rubber band stretches with increasing weight.

STRETCH GRAPH (1) ◯   Graphing ( )

1. String a "bucket handle" on a tin can. Hang it from a rubber band chained to paper clips firmly taped to your table edge.

JUST OVER EDGE

RUBBER BAND

STRING HANDLE

2. Number lines (not spaces), on a sheet of notebook paper. Suspend it from thread so the rim of the can meets the top zero line.

RIM MEETS "0" LINE

THREAD

TAPE

3. Add water, 1 large test tube at a time. Record where the rim of the can meets the lined paper. Display your results in a table.

4. Graph your results

5. Hook's law states that the ratio of stretch to weight is constant if the rubber band is perfectly elastic. Does your rubber band obey Hook's law? Explain.

WEIGHT (test tubes of water)	STRETCH (number of ruled lines)
0	0
1	
2	
3	

© 1990 by TOPS Learning Systems   13

Answers / Notes

3-4. Measurements will vary widely according to the capacity of the can, the size of the rubber band and its elasticity. Students should estimate between the lines of notebook paper recording values to the nearest tenth of a line. Here is one result:

5. Parts of the graph line are nearly straight. This means that y/x (the ratio of stretch to weight) is the same for each point in the straight part of the graph—that the rubber band obeys Hook's law at least during part of its stretching. *In this example, the graph line curves slightly (becomes non-proportional) at the extremes, when it is stretched very little or stretched a whole lot.*

WEIGHT	STRETCH
0	0
1	.7
2	1.8
3	3.1
4	4.4
5	5.9
6	7.8
7	9.6
8	11.4
9	13.2
10	15.0
11	16.8
12	18.2
13	19.7
14	21.1
15	22.4
16	23.7

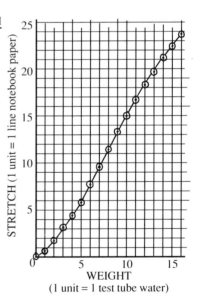

STRETCH (1 unit = 1 line notebook paper)

WEIGHT
(1 unit = 1 test tube water)

Materials

☐ A tin can. Punch holes on opposite sides near the rim, so students can tie in a string handle. The string may also be attached securely with masking tape if each end is taped twice: Tape the first piece so the end of the string remains free. Turn this free end up over the first piece of tape, and tape it a second time.

☐ A rubber band of medium thickness and length. Use only high-quality rubber bands with strong new rubber. The ones you find wrapped around newspapers are suitable. Test one in advance to make sure it easily supports a can filled with water. All rubber bands should have roughly uniform dimensions to facilitate easy comparisons in the next activity.

☐ String for the "bucket handle" and thread to hang the notebook paper.

☐ A large test tube, or equivalent. Our particular test tube was 15 cm long and held 29 ml of water.

☐ A water source. A large bucket of water resting on newspaper spread on the floor facilitates economy of movement and easy clean-up.

☐ Paper clips.
☐ Masking tape.
☐ Lined notebook paper.
☐ Graph paper.

(TO) investigate how rubber bands stretch differently when paired in series and in parallel.

STRETCH GRAPH (2) ◯   Graphing (   )

1. Predict how your stretch graph might change if you use 2 rubber bands (instead of just 1), connected like these:

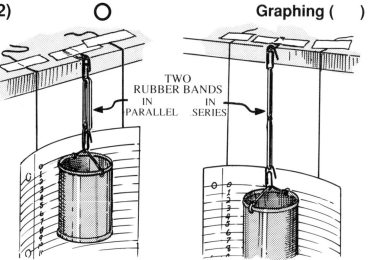

TWO RUBBER BANDS IN PARALLEL — IN SERIES

First sketch how 1 rubber band stretched, then draw how the 2 rubber bands might stretch differently. Give reasons for each answer.

2. Test your prediction. Make a data table for both pairs of rubber bands, then plot your results on the same graph as the previous activity.

14

Answers / Notes

1. Two rubber bands connected in parallel only stretch half as far as one because each supports half the weight of the water. Hence, the graph whould rise half as fast with the addition of each test tube of water.

Two rubber bands connected in series stretch twice as far as one, because each one supports the entire weight of the water. Hence, the graph should rise twice as fast with the addition of each test tube of water.

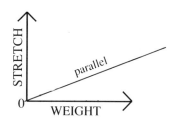

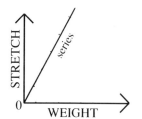

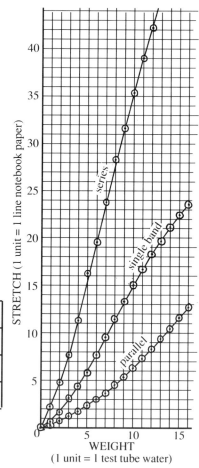

STRETCH (1 unit = 1 line notebook paper)

WEIGHT
(1 unit = 1 test tube water)

2.

WEIGHT (test tubes of water)		0	1	2	3	4	5	6	7	8	9	10	11	12	13	14	15	16
STRETCH (number of ruled lines)	SINGLE band	0	.7	1.8	3.1	4.4	5.9	7.8	9.6	11.4	13.2	15.0	16.8	18.2	19.7	21.1	22.4	23.7
	2 bands in PARALLEL	0	.3	.8	1.2	1.8	2.3	3.0	3.7	4.5	5.3	6.2	7.2	8.2	9.3	10.4	11.6	12.8
	2 bands in SERIES	0	2.2	4.9	7.8	11.2	16.2	19.5	23.9	28.2	31.7	35.3	39.0	42.2	45.2	48.2	51.0	

Materials
☐ Use the same materials as in the previous activity.

(TO) map ordered pairs from one coordinate system onto another. To understand how the shape and size of a graph is altered by changing its scale.

FUNNY FLOWER ◯ Graphing (   )

1. Transform the flower you graphed in the beginning task card. To do this:
   a. Double the length of each unit on the x-axis, but leave the y-axis scale unchanged.
   b. Map (transfer) each ordered pair from the old scale to the new scale.

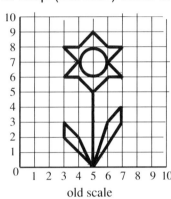

old scale

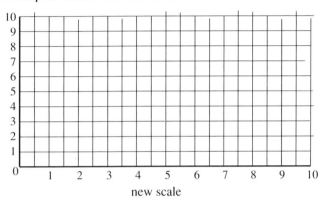

new scale

2. How would you make your flower …
   a. look tall and narrow?   b. have an area 4 times as large?

15

Answers / Notes

1.

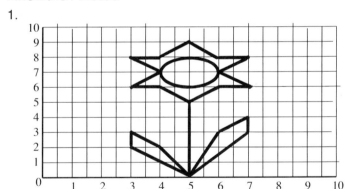

2a. Stretch out the y-axis scale but keep leave the x-axis unchanged. (Or compress the x-axis scale but leave the y-axis unchanged.)

2b. Double the scales on both the x and y axis. This makes an image with 4 times as much area.

Materials

☐ The flower graph coordinates from task 1.
☐ Graph paper.
☐ A straight edge.

(TO) map ordered pairs onto a novel coordinate system of each student's own design. To appreciate how the shape of a graph is distorted by changing its coordinate system.

CRAZY GRAPH ⃝ Graphing ( )

1. Draw your own crazy graph paper design and number the lines. Use one of these grid patterns or invent your own.

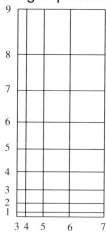 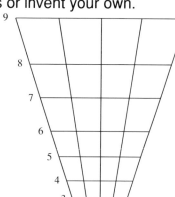 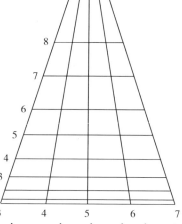

2. Twist the original flower into a new shape by mapping each ordered pair onto your new graph paper.

16

Answers / Notes

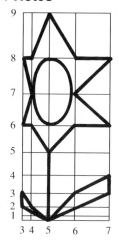 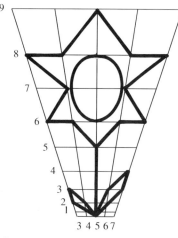 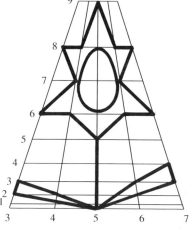

To construct these 3 grids, first draw the horizontal lines: *lay down a base line; construct the next line 3mm above this base; the next 6 mm above the second, the next 9 cm above the third, and so on. Then draw in the proper vertical lines pertaining to each grid:*

In the first grid above, the spacings between each vertical grid begins with a 6 mm interval and increase by 6 mm moving right.

In the second and third grids above, the top and bottom horizontal lines measure 15 mm and 3 mm. Center these so they "T" into a middle vertical line. Join the ends with 2 more near-vertical lines. Subdivide the 2 columns formed with 2 more near-vertical lines to form a total of 4 columns in each grid.

Materials

☐ A metric ruler.
☐ The flower graph coordinates from task 1.

(TO) map ordered pairs onto circular graph paper. To discover that a circular mirror transforms the circular figure back to rectangular dimensions.

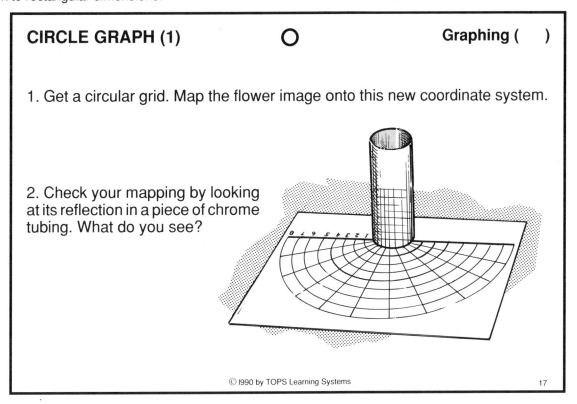

CIRCLE GRAPH (1)   O   Graphing (   )

1. Get a circular grid. Map the flower image onto this new coordinate system.

2. Check your mapping by looking at its reflection in a piece of chrome tubing. What do you see?

© 1990 by TOPS Learning Systems   17

Answers / Notes

1-2. The distorted flower appears normal when reflected back from the circular mirror.

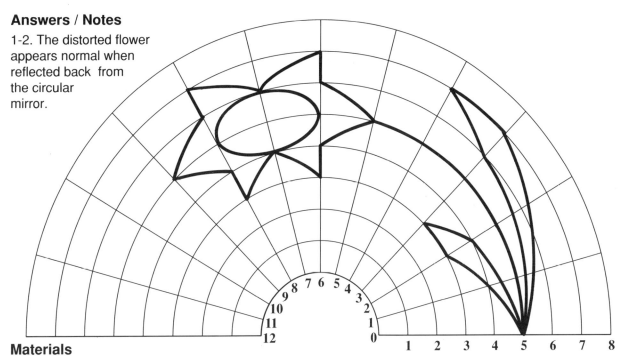

Materials

☐ Circular graph paper. Make 2 photocopies of the supplementary circular grid at the back of this book. Combine both images, 2-up, on a standard-sized sheet of copy paper. Run off at least 2 copies of this 2-up image for each student in your class. Only 1 grid is needed now, but 2 or 3 more will be used in the next two activities.

☐ The flower graph coordinates from task 1.

☐ Chrome-plated tubing at least one inch in diameter or larger. You can find this in the plumbing section of your local hardware store. A shiny stainless steel mixing bowl may also work if it has a sufficiently small diameter.

(TO) map simple geometric figures onto circular graph paper so their images, reflected from a circular mirror, appear normal.

CIRCLE GRAPH (2) ○ Graphing (   )

1. Make an 8 x 12 rectangular grid with 2 squares per number. Draw a simple image (your choice) on this grid.

2. Now map your figure onto circular graph paper. Check your mapping by viewing its reflection in a circular mirror. What should you see?

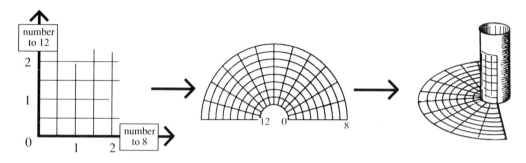

3. Spell out your name, or initials, on another 8 x 12 rectangular grid and repeat the experiment.

18

Answers / Notes

1-2. Here is how a square with diagonals looks on both grids. Students should report that their image, whatever they have drawn, appears normal in a circular mirror.

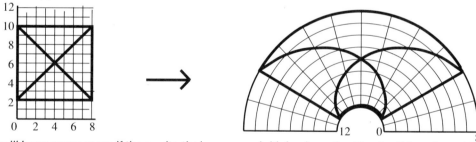

3. Students will have more room if they write their name or initials along the Y-axis. If they forget to reverse the lettering, for normal viewing in a circular mirror, they should repeat the experiment. Treat these false starts as learning experiences, not mistakes.

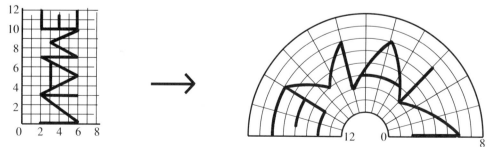

Materials

☐ Normal rectangular graph paper.
☐ Circular graph paper reproduced in the previous activity.
☐ Chrome-plated tubing.

(TO) select suitable scales for a population graph. To appreciate how doubling population growth "explodes" off the graph.

DOUBLE GROW GRAPH   ◯   Graphing (   )

1. There are about 6 billion people living on our planet, and the population is increasing at a rate that doubles about every 30 years. Assuming this rate of growth continues, make a population table for the next 300 years.

years	population (billions)
0	6
30	12
60	24
⋮	⋮
300	

2. Graph of this population growth.

3. Does your graph show that overpopulation is a serious world problem? Explain.

19

Answers / Notes

1.

Year	Population (billions)
0	6
30	12
60	24
90	48
120	96
150	192
180	384
210	768
240	1536
270	3072
300	6144

3. Yes. If present growth rates continued over the next 300 years, the population would increase 1000 fold to about 4 trillion people. This huge number far exceeds the earth's capacity to support life.

2.
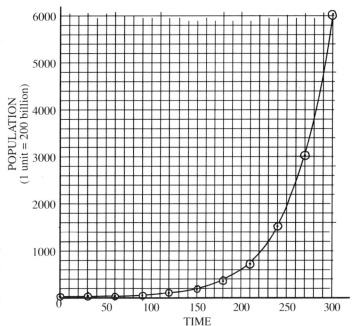

Materials

☐ Graph paper.

(TO) graph birth rate and total population for a family of mice. To compare the environmental impact of mice with human beings.

A FAMILY OF MICE ○ Graphing ( )

A pair of mice give birth, on average, to a litter of 6 young every 20 days. If these young, in turn, reach sexual maturity and mate after 100 days, how many mice will be in the family of 1 pair after 360 days (1 year).

1. Use graph paper to keep track of births.

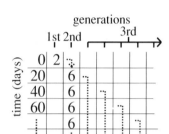

2. Graph the number of *new births* every 20 days. Draw a second line to show *total population*.

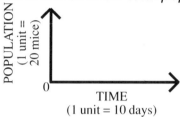

3. Which presents the greater stress to our environment and its natural resources, a population explosion of mice or humans? Explain.

20

Answers / Notes

1. *This 1-year table assumes no deaths in the population plus 100% mate availability and reproductive success.*

time	1st	2nd	3rd		
0	2				
20	6				
40	6				
60	6				
80	6				
100	6				
120	6				
140	6	18			
160	6	18 18			
180	6	18 18 18			
200	6	18 18 18 18			
220	6	18 18 18 18 18			
240	6	18 18 18 18 18 18			
260	6	18 18 18 18 18 18 18		54	
280	6	18 18 18 18 18 18 18 18		54 54	
300	6	18 18 18 18 18 18 18 18 18		54 54 54	
320	6	18 18 18 18 18 18 18 18 18 18		54 54 54 54	
340	6	18 18 18 18 18 18 18 18 18 18 18		54 54 54 54 54	
360	6	18 18 18 18 18 18 18 18 18 18 18 18		54 54 54 54 54 54	

2.
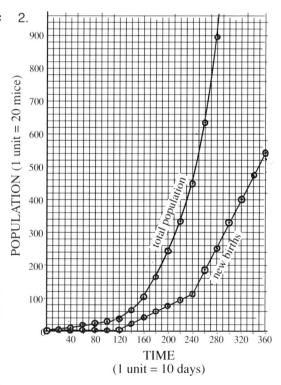

3. Mice live in ecological harmony with their surroundings, consuming only what they need. Their population is held in check by natural predation as they, in turn, become food for other animals higher in the food chain. Humans, by contrast, have few natural predators, so their population continues to explode. They further stress the environment by living in ecological disharmony — consuming more than they need; returning pollution, garbage and toxic waste to their environment. Unlike mice, humans can consciously choose to live differently and exercise self restraint.

Materials

☐ Graph paper.

notes 20   enrichment

REPRODUCIBLE
STUDENT
TASK CARDS

Task Cards Options

Here are 3 management options to consider before you photocopy:

1. Consumable Worksheets: Copy 1 complete set of task card pages. Cut out each card and fix it to a separate sheet of boldly lined paper. Duplicate a class set of each worksheet master you have made, 1 per student. Direct students to follow the task card instructions at the top of each page, then respond to questions in the lined space underneath.

2. Nonconsumable Reference Booklets: Copy and collate the 2-up task card pages in sequence. Make perhaps half as many sets as the students who will use them. Staple each set in the upper left corner, both front and back to prevent the outside pages from working loose. Tell students that these task card booklets are for reference only. They should use them as they would any textbook, responding to questions on their own papers, returning them unmarked and in good shape at the end of the module.

3. Nonconsumable Task Cards: Copy several sets of task card pages. Laminate them, if you wish, for extra durability, then cut out each card to display in your room. You might pin cards to bulletin boards; or punch out the holes and hang them from wall hooks (you can fashion hooks from paper clips and tape these to the wall); or fix cards to cereal boxes with paper fasteners, 4 to a box; or keep cards on designated reference tables. The important thing is to provide enough task card reference points about your classroom to avoid a jam of too many students at any one location. Two or 3 task card sets should accommodate everyone, since different students will use different cards at different times.

ORDERED PAIRS (1) ○ Graphing (   )

1. Draw X and Y coordinates on graph paper. Number alternate lines out to 10 as shown.

2. Plot the ordered pairs listed in each table. Connect points, working down from the top of each table.

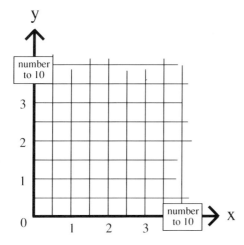

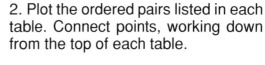

(a)		(b)	
x	y	x	y
5	5	5	9
5	0	4	8
4	2	3	8
3	3	4	7
3	2	3	6
5	0	4	6
6	3	5	5
7	4	6	6
7	3	7	6
5	0	6	7
		7	8
		6	8
		5	9

(c) Make a circle with the center at (5,7) and a radius of 1.

3. What have you drawn?

© 1990 by TOPS Learning Systems

1

ORDERED PAIRS (2) ○ Graphing (   )

Draw these 4 coordinate systems (as scaled) on 1 sheet of graph paper. *Plot* and *circle* the ordered pairs in each table. Connect your points with a smooth line, but don't draw inside the circles.

1.

x	y
0	0
20	2.7
40	4.3
60	5.2
80	5.8
100	5.9

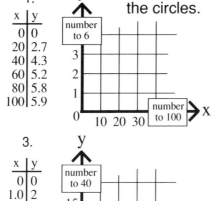

2.

x	y
0	0
.5	.62
1.0	1.25
1.5	1.82
2.0	2.50
2.5	3.17

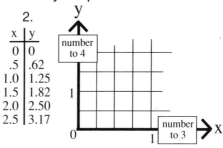

3.

x	y
0	0
1.0	2
2.0	6
3.0	13
4.0	24
4.5	35

4.

x	y
0	0
.7	.8
2.5	2.2
5.1	3.0
6.6	3.0
8.8	3.6
10.2	4.3

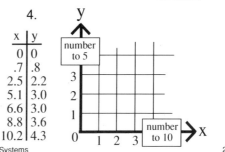

© 1990 by TOPS Learning Systems

2

BOOK LEAVES (1)   O   Graphing (   )

1. Select a book with at least 200 leaves (400 pages). Complete the data table by counting leaves and measuring their thickness in millimeters. Estimate between the lines to the nearest 0.1 mm.

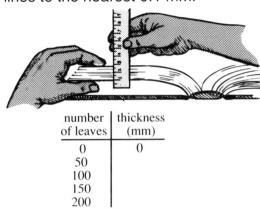

number of leaves	thickness (mm)
0	0
50	
100	
150	
200	

2. Plot and circle each ordered pair. Connect your points with a straight line, but don't draw inside the circles.

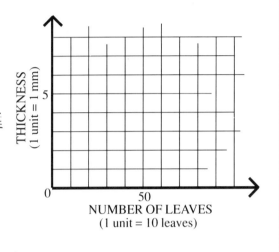

THICKNESS (1 unit = 1 mm)

NUMBER OF LEAVES (1 unit = 10 leaves)

3

BOOK LEAVES (2)   O   Graphing (   )

1. Read from your graph the number of leaves in 10.0 mm. Check your answer by counting book leaves. How do your answers compare?

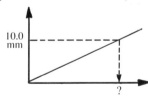

3. Divide 2 index cards into 25 rectangles each. Stack them to form a flat, even edge, then rubber-band them together.

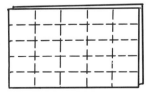

50 LAYERS

2. Read from your graph the thickness of 25 leaves. Check your answer by actual measurement. How do your answers compare?

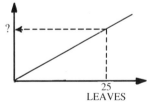

25 LEAVES

4. Plot and label a graph line for index cards on your book-leaves graph. Extrapolate (extend) the line past 50 leaves.

5. How is the slope (steepness) of the graph line related to paper thickness?

4

EXTRAPOLATING BOOK LEAVES ⭕ Graphing ( )

1. Draw a new graph with a scale that is 5 times smaller. Plot the same points you measured in activities 3 and 4.

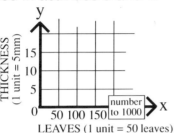

2. Extrapolate your graph lines out to 1000 leaves. Use thread to help you judge the best direction. Label both graph lines.

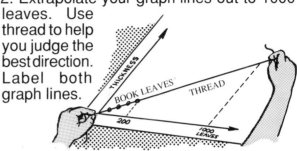

3. Read your graph to find the thickness of 1000 book leaves and 1000 index cards.

4. Check each answer by solving these proportions. Why don't your extrapolations exactly agree with your calculations?

BOOK LEAVES

$$\frac{200 \text{ leaves}}{\text{thickness}} = \frac{1000 \text{ leaves}}{?}$$
└─ *(Use measurement from activity 3.)*

INDEX CARD

$$\frac{50 \text{ leaves}}{\text{thickness}} = \frac{1000 \text{ leaves}}{?}$$
└─ *(Use measurement from activity 4.)*

5

CONTAINER CURVES (1) ⭕ Graphing ( )

1. Cut out 2 metric rulers. Fix 1 each to a 100 ml graduate and a 100 ml beaker resting on a flat surface.

a. Trim excess ruler off the top …

b. Fix the back of the ruler to the glass with masking tape rolled sticky side out …

c. Add just enough water to form a water line., Fix "0" on the ruler over this line.

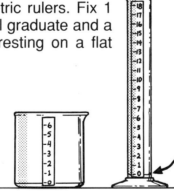

2. Pour large test tubes full of water into each container. Record the height of the water level after each addition in a data table.

3. Plot your data for both containers onto the same graph. Label each graph line.

4. Why is the slope of one graph line steeper than the other?

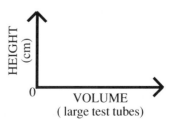

6

CONTAINER CURVES (2)　　O　　　　　　　　Graphing (　　)

1. Collect containers shaped like those below.

2. Tape rulers to the sides of each one as before. Record how the water level rises in each container as you add test tubes of water. Graph your results.

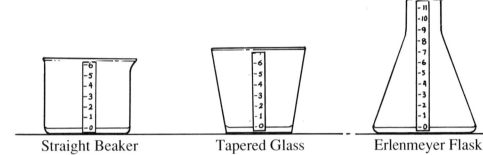

Straight Beaker　　　　　Tapered Glass　　　　　Erlenmeyer Flask

3. Explain how the graph line of each container is determined by its three-dimensional shape.

7

CONTAINER CURVES (3)　　O　　　　　　　　Graphing (　　)

1. Set up 100 ml beakers like these. Make the ball out of clay. Roll it to fit inside the beaker with about 1/2 cm to spare.

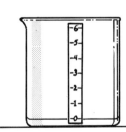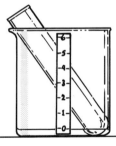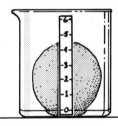

No Object　　　　　Large Test Tube　　　　　Clay Ball

2. What shape do you think the graph lines will take as you fill these containers? Draw your best guess *before* you experiment.

3. Now do the experiment. This time add small test tubes of water, in place of large ones. Evaluate your prediction.

8

SQUARES OF WATER ⭕ Graphing (   )

1. Graph each shape on the same grid. (Hint: Think about adding "squares" of water.)

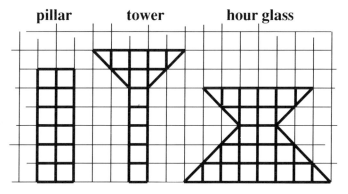

pillar   tower   hour glass

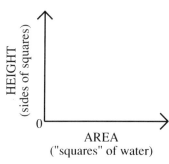

HEIGHT (sides of squares)

0

AREA ("squares" of water)

2. Explain how your graph lines indicate...
   a. the tallest shape.
   b. the largest shape.
   c. a narrowing shape.
   d. a widening shape.
   e. a uniform shape.

9

WHAT'S THE POINT? ⭕ Graphing (   )

1a. Divide the y coordinate of each point by it x coordinate (y/x). List your results.

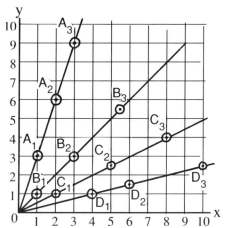

1b. If points lie on the same straight line, what seems true?

2a. Find the ratio of coordinates (y/x) for each point on these curves. List your results.

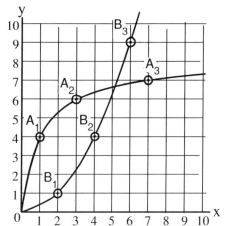

2b. What can you conclude?

10

DIRECTLY PROPORTIONAL? ○   Graphing (   )

1. Decide by graphing if the side of a square is directly proportional to its...

...area.			...perimeter.	
LENGTH (sides)	AREA (squares)		LENGTH (sides)	PERIMETER (sides)
1	1 □		1	4 □
2	4 ⊞		2	8 ⊞
3	9		3	12
4	16		4	16

2. What can you conclude?

PI GRAPH   ○   Graphing (   )

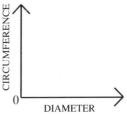

1. Measure the diameter and circumference of 4 different cylinders. Use bottles, cans, lids or other circular objects.

2. Complete this data table. Draw a straight line between your points, using thread to help you determine its best placement.

kind of CYLINDER	DIAMETER (cm)	CIRCUMFERENCE (cm)

3. What is the ratio of coordinates (C/d) for all points on this line? Explain.

4. These equations are famous in geometry: $\pi = C/d$, $C = \pi d$, $d = C/\pi$. What do they mean?

STRETCH GRAPH (1)   O   Graphing (   )

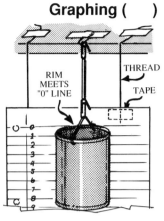

1. String a "bucket handle" on a tin can. Hang it from a rubber band chained to paper clips firmly taped to your table edge.

JUST OVER EDGE

RUBBER BAND

STRING HANDLE

2. Number lines (not spaces), on a sheet of notebook paper. Suspend it from thread so the rim of the can meets the top zero line.

RIM MEETS "0" LINE

THREAD

TAPE

3. Add water, 1 large test tube at a time. Record where the rim of the can meets the lined paper. Display your results in a table.

4. Graph your results

5. Hook's law states that the ratio of stretch to weight is constant if the rubber band is perfectly elastic. Does your rubber band obey Hook's law? Explain.

WEIGHT (test tubes of water)	STRETCH (number of ruled lines)
0	0
1	
2	
3	

13

STRETCH GRAPH (2)   O   Graphing (   )

1. Predict how your stretch graph might change if you use 2 rubber bands (instead of just 1), connected like these:

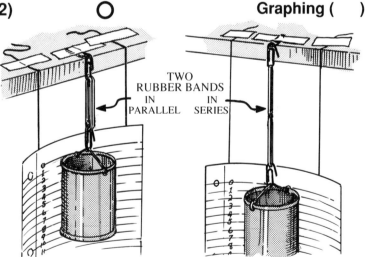

TWO RUBBER BANDS IN PARALLEL

IN SERIES

First sketch how 1 rubber band stretched, then draw how the 2 rubber bands might stretch differently. Give reasons for each answer.

2. Test your prediction. Make a data table for both pairs of rubber bands, then plot your results on the same graph as the previous activity.

14

FUNNY FLOWER **Graphing ( )**

1. Transform the flower you graphed in the beginning task card. To do this:
   a. Double the length of each unit on the x-axis, but leave the y-axis scale unchanged.
   b. Map (transfer) each ordered pair from the old scale to the new scale.

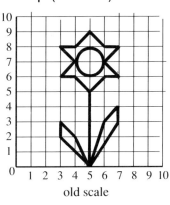
old scale

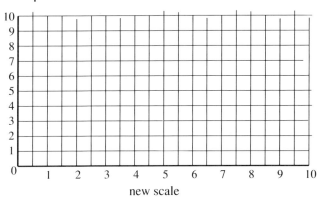
new scale

2. How would you make your flower …
   a. look tall and narrow?   b. have an area 4 times as large?

15

CRAZY GRAPH **Graphing ( )**

1. Draw your own crazy graph paper design and number the lines. Use one of these grid patterns or invent your own.

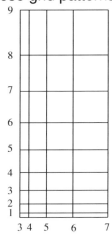 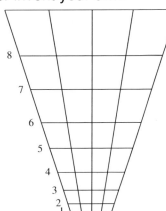 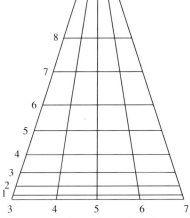

2. Twist the original flower into a new shape by mapping each ordered pair onto your new graph paper.

16

CIRCLE GRAPH (1)   Graphing (   )

1. Get a circular grid. Map the flower image onto this new coordinate system.

2. Check your mapping by looking at its reflection in a piece of chrome tubing. What do you see?

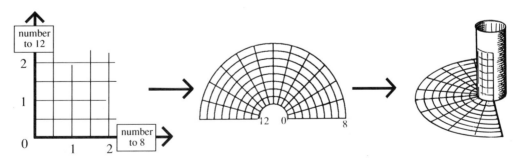

17

CIRCLE GRAPH (2)   Graphing (   )

1. Make an 8 x 12 rectangular grid with 2 squares per number. Draw a simple image (your choice) on this grid.

2. Now map your figure onto circular graph paper. Check your mapping by viewing its reflection in a circular mirror. What should you see?

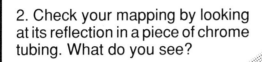

3. Spell out your name, or initials, on another 8 x 12 rectangular grid and repeat the experiment.

18

DOUBLE GROW GRAPH Graphing (   )

1. There are about 6 billion people living on our planet, and the population is increasing at a rate that doubles about every 30 years. Assuming this rate of growth continues, make a population table for the next 300 years.

years	population (billions)
0	6
30	12
60	24
⋮	⋮
300	

2. Graph of this population growth.

3. Does your graph show that overpopulation is a serious world problem? Explain.

19

A FAMILY OF MICE Graphing (   )

A pair of mice give birth, on average, to a litter of 6 young every 20 days. If these young, in turn, reach sexual maturity and mate after 100 days, how many mice will be in the family of 1 pair after 360 days (1 year).

1. Use graph paper to keep track of births.

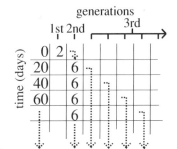

2. Graph the number of *new births* every 20 days. Draw a second line to show *total population*.

3. Which presents the greater stress to our environment and its natural resources, a population explosion of mice or humans? Explain.

20

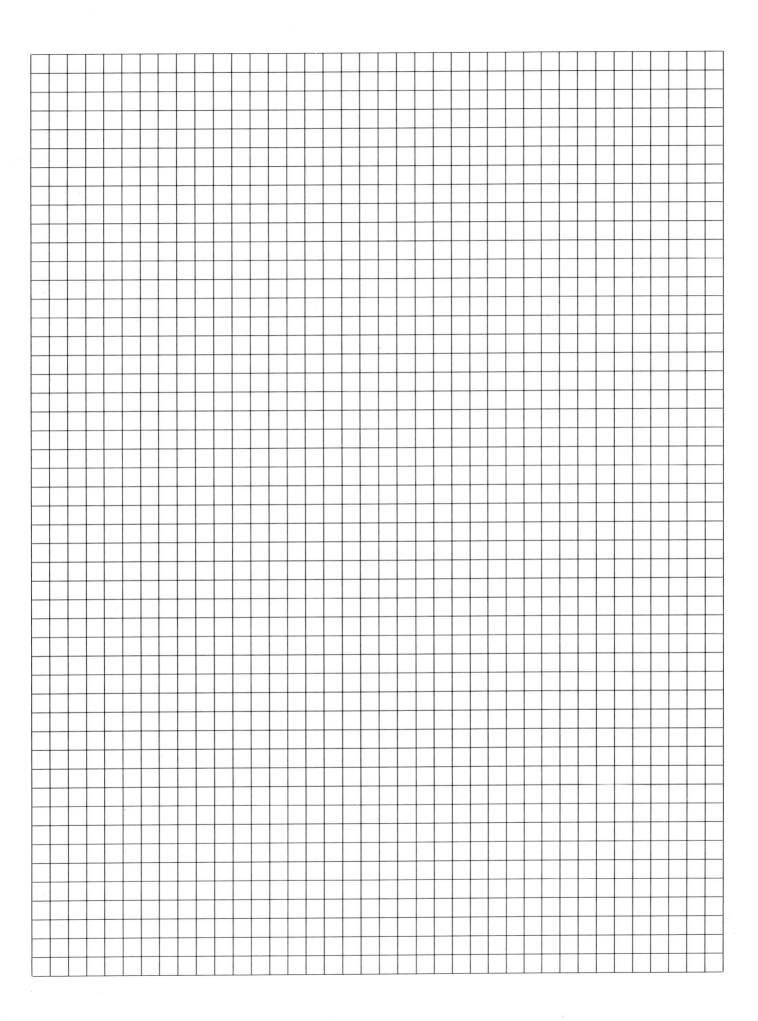

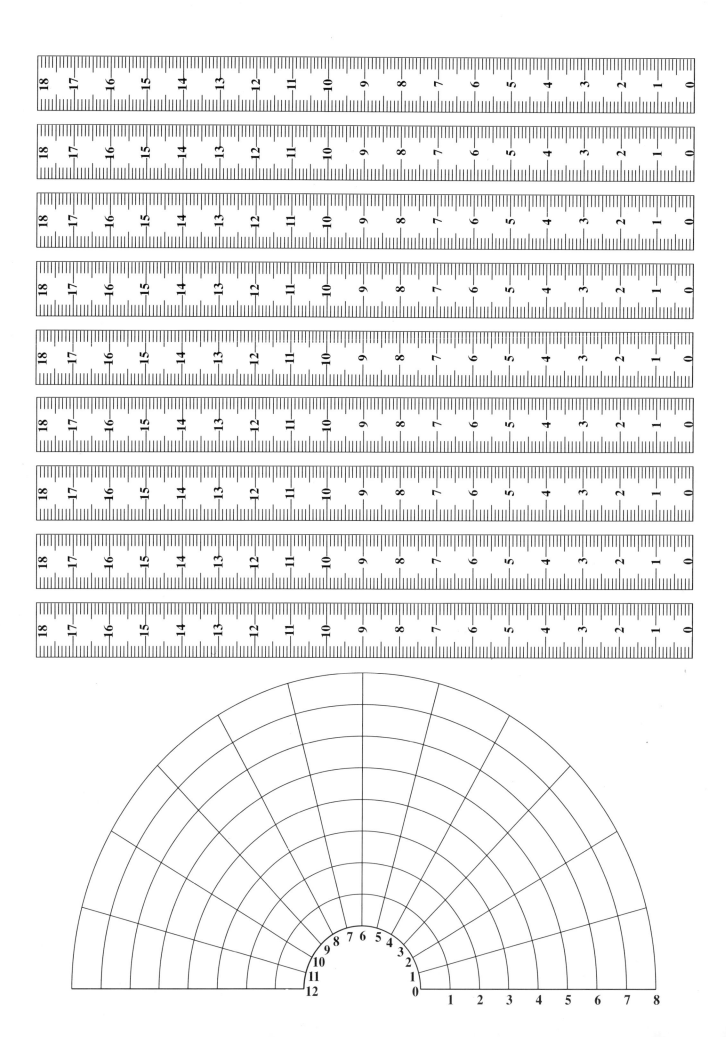